FROM PAIN TO PURPOSE

FROM SPECIAL EDUCATION TEACHER TO KINGDOM TEACHER

CHAVON ANETTE
FIRE LEADERSHIP COACH

Copyright © 2022 by Chavon Thomas

ISBN: 978-0-578-28167-4

Cover Design: iambiancabrown.com

Printed in the USA:

All rights reserved. No part of this book may be reproduced or used in any manner without written permission of the copyright owner except for the use of quotations in a book review. For more information, address: www.chavonanette.com

This book is dedicated to Power and Grace Leaders Inc. Movement, the coaches, clients, and students who went through Powerhouse Leaders University, Power and Grace Leaders Inc. executive team, and the mentors, coaches, friends, and family who supported me in my journey pursuing God and His purpose for my life.

Tienisha Earl:

"Chavon Anette, your ministry and business have helped me get to the next level of elevation. You have helped me step up and out when I simply wanted to shrink, and for that, I truly thank you for your hard work and dedication."

Chante Smith:

"I'm so grateful to you, Chavon, for your YES. I have learned to trust again and allow myself to have real kingdom sisters because of you. These days are imperative when it comes to connecting with the people God has lined up to take you to your next. You are truly a gem, and your transparency and heart to help others are unparalleled to what I've experienced before. Your courage to press through when it hurts is not something you see often. You are a woman of virtue and integrity. Truly one of the best leaders the Kingdom of God is blessed to have."

Rebekah Detox Dandy:

"Chavon is a true prayer warrior who speaks life into the women God calls us to be!!! I'm so blessed to have her as a spiritual coach in her Women of Purpose mentorship program and for the time in fellowship and service with her large community."

Dr. Charlene D. Winley:

"Chavon, your courage and obedience enabled me to take quantum leaps both professionally and personally. Continue walking in DIVINE obedience. You're a movement for such a time as this."

Kelly Asheim:

"I'm so thankful for Chavon. She came into my life a year ago, and I have grown so much spiritually. I am growing in gifts I didn't even know I had until Chavon spoke into my life."

Erin Pitt:

"You've impacted and blessed the lives of so many people. And for that, God's heart and hand will continue to be extended towards you.

Chavon, you've been a connector, a coach, and a blueprint since our paths crossed. I'm privileged to glean and be empowered to champion my own trail to greatness."

Table of Contents:

Introduction	**9**
Part I I had no Idea	**16**
Chapter 1 Life as a Special Educator	17
Chapter 2 The struggle to Balance it All	23
Chapter 3 The Year I Found Me	27
Chapter 4 Unexpected Pain and Heartache	31
Part II He Knows Best	**38**
Chapter 5 God, I say Yes	39
Chapter 6 The Valley of Decisions	49
Part III The Journey Filled with Miracles	**52**
Chapter 7 Walking by Faith	53
Chapter 8 The writing on the Wall	59
Chapter 9 Purpose, Pain, Promise	63
Epilogue	**67**
Meet the Author:	**71**

Foreword
Dr. Shameika Dean

Not everyone knows how to triumph through trials and tragedy, but in this book, Chavon transcribes what it looks like tangibly. She details a very personal journey of complete surrender to the call of God on your life and how success will show up when you do. If you have been faced with the unimaginable and looking for a formula to defeat fear, this book is for you. If you are looking to understand your purpose, this book is for you. If you want to know how to defeat the odds and the opposition that are stacked against you, this book is for you. If you are looking for tools to transform your life, this book is for you.

When you're done reading this book, you will be inspired and have instructions to implement, and you'll know what to do to see an increase in every area of your life. I am honored to be chosen to do the forward because I have personally witnessed the evolution of Chavon Thomas. She is the epitome of perseverance and walking in your God-given purpose.

Introduction

April 2, 2021, I took this giant leap one year ago to release this book. I stopped living the life that I was expected to live and took a chance on God as I left my job as a special education teacher in the education system. I decided that struggling to meet the demands that COVID brought while fulfilling my purpose was unbearable. I took a chance on God, and I decided to bet on myself. However, what is to be said that on the brink of life-changing years are also days filled with tears and sorrow. What is to be said about a vision that looks so exciting is to be met with great challenges and obstacles beyond comprehension. Let's take a moment and allow me to rewind time to the year 2020.

"How could we be starting a year with a loss that brought pain to so many people worldwide?"

First, there was a news update: Kobe Bryant and his daughter passed in a helicopter crash along with others. I remember hearing the news and sitting in my one-bedroom apartment on my large grey couch in utter shock and tears falling down my face. 2020 was the year so many people were excited about. How could we be starting the year with a loss that brought pain to so many people around the world? The world felt the pain of losing a hero, a role model, a voice of change, and a man of strength and determination despite all flaws. I asked God why this happened. I had no idea that the loss of someone I only admired from a distance would affect me so profoundly. Surely that would be the biggest hurdle of my life in 2020; I was wrong.

"I was trying to figure out how this was all possible."

A few months later, I walked into my job in the English wing of the building through the double doors like it was a normal day. I was looking forward to the sea of blue lockers as my feet touched the ground on the long black mat at the entrance and ready to celebrate the boys' basketball team making it to the next round to begin their quest for the state championship. However, I was greeted by a fellow educator and told that a former student and basketball player who celebrated with us at the game and just graduated a year prior had died. Immediately, I screamed in agony, tears ran down my face, and I fell to the ground, unable to get up. I was trying to figure out how this was all possible. I had just seen him celebrating the win with the boys at the game. God, what was going on? This death wrecked me, and I just knew it would be the last because this one was close to home.

Then, on March 13th, my wedding anniversary, the schools closed because of the rise of people being infected by the COVID virus. We heard alarming numbers of the rate of people passing from this virus, and we were on a nationwide shutdown. Fear of getting a virus that had the potential to take you or your loved ones away from this world was horrifying. All we could do was try and get necessities from the grocery store like water, toilet paper, bread, and food, and there were so many shelves empty of these items because of fear. With a worldwide crisis on our hands, this felt like it was enough, but that was not the final crisis of 2020 for me.

"Fear of getting a virus that had the potential to take you or your loved ones away from this world was horrifying."

Fast forward a few months later, my husband and I came home from being with friends on Mother's Day with subs from WaWa, and he answered the phone, dropped his food on the futon in our one-bedroom apartment, and there was sheer terror in his eyes that I had never seen before. It frightened me to my core. He received a call from his mom that his little sister, my sister-in-law, Lexus Thomas, had died in a car crash driven by her abusive ex-boyfriend. After all those losses in 2020, what would we do? This loss was unbelievable. This loss put me in a state of shock. This loss brought anger and great confusion. God, my husband and I love you and pray for our family members, so how is this possible? Intense pain, call to friends, sleepless nights, travel to Rhode Island, and attempts not to cave in under pressure. What do you do? How do you respond? How do you keep building?

"This loss was unbelievable."

I prayed; I stayed focused; I continued the plan; I looked for God in all things and cried. There were times when a certain loss in my life and challenges made me wonder how in the world am I not a ball of mush? To be honest, I know it is not by my power in the slightest. God has held me up. God has been my strong tower. God has been my place of refuge and strength.

As I write this introduction, all I can do as tears fill my eyes is thank God because he held me close. Let me tell you, the journey of purpose is not for the faint-hearted. The level of challenges that you endure is great, but there is a rainbow of promise on the other side of your pain. I always say, "You have to get through the horror of your story to get to the beauty of your destiny." There were also challenges that I was managing internally during all these external losses. The challenges of my health, financial difficulties, marriage tension, and more were compounding in my life. There were many days of tears and screams covered in silence.

Nevertheless, my hope was in Christ, and I had full belief that the plan and purpose of my life were about to break forth. The vision of God for my life and the love of God for me surpassed the things that could have killed and made me forfeit my destiny. How did I continue?

In this book, I will be as transparent and vulnerable as the Lord allows me to be because I want people of God to understand that although this journey is not easy, it's both necessary and worth it.

Let's rewind a little farther to 2019 before we dive into the meat of this book.

Where did I get the strength to build in 2020 despite all the pain and loss that impacted my life? It began in 2019. I found myself being a leader who was bleeding. You know how everyone says don't be that person? Well, I was that person. So, grace to you sis or bro, if you are in that state, and I pray that my story inspires you.

By 2019, I had authored many books and spoke to empower and encourage others, but it felt like life was killing me. I was doing my best to be a good wife, church member, friend, and coworker, and the weight of it all exacerbated me. How could the weight of the reality of the things I was carrying turn around for my good? God has a good way of bringing all the suppressed things to rise to the surface. I had to deal with my lack of identity. Who was I apart from being everything for everyone? That reflective questioning allowed me to find out who I truly was. I needed to understand that my identity was not in what I could do or be for everyone else, but it was in just being a daughter of God. I had to understand that it was sonship or daughtership (yeah, I know it's not a word) that I needed to embrace fully.

This was nothing that I had to work for. In accepting Jesus as savior, I am adopted into the best family with the best daddy in the world, my Abba father. In this new identity, I no longer have to perform or wear a mask to cover up my past or present hard realities, but I could instead be honest and transparent with myself and others. I am enough with him even in my imperfections.

I was an educator in the Virginia Beach City Public Schools system. I loved teaching and motivating students. However, the responsibilities that come with being a special education teacher are great regarding paperwork, and during COVID, the challenges only persisted. I understood that what I loved the most was not the paperwork but teaching, motivating, and inspiring the students I encountered. I even wrote a book for teens in my local area to be more aware of what it would take to be successful and make the most of their time in high school as they prepared for their futures.

However, after a while, my passion for the things God called me to do outside of being an educator began to grow. There was a new path that God was directing me on. Interesting, after three years of being a teacher and five years in the school system, I heard God telling me that I would not be doing it too much longer.

When I heard him say that to me, I was excited and nervous. I was excited at the thought of God allowing me to travel the world and preach because I had not stepped into Entrepreneurship yet. Yes, I was nervous about leaving the path that I spent years and earned big money in debt pursuing. My parents taught me to go to college and get a job I could work for life. The vision was to be a doctor or lawyer, but the same rules applied to being an educator.

There were always high expectations placed on me since I did well in school, and I also placed high expectations on myself. However, it's more important to me to be who God has called me to be over what others want me to be or how I should be for others to be proud of me.

A lot has transpired over the last year after leaving my steady job as an educator during a global pandemic. I will talk about my journey, but I had to give you some background before we jump in.

Three things I want you to remember from reading my journey.

1. God is Faithful to His Promises.
2. God is not a respecter of persons, so he can do great things in your life also.
3. God has a plan for your life too, and he is more committed to your purpose than you are.

Join me on this journey.... Let's keep going!

PART I
I had no Idea

FROM PAIN TO PURPOSE

CHAVON ANETTE

Chapter 1
Life as a Special Educator

As I grew up, so many great employment ideas went through my mind: being a Just for Me model, becoming a doctor, becoming a lawyer, and becoming a math teacher. I did well in school as a kid growing up in school, so my expectations were high. In the anthology *Undeterred*, I talk about my unorthodox journey to become a teacher. After getting my bachelor's degree in history with a minor in English, I planned to be a teacher assistant, where I prepared to go to Law School. However, instead, I transitioned from being a teacher assistant to taking courses to get a provisional teaching license and later obtaining a master's degree in teaching with an emphasis in Special Education. We can have many plans in life, but I learned to allow God to direct my footsteps. As a teacher, I had the opportunity to impact the lives of so many students.

God truly blessed me on the journey to becoming an educator. I was told that not many people received a job as a teacher on a provisional (temporary) license unless they had special connections in the school system. After my second year as a teacher assistant, I finished the course work to obtain the provisional license, but it did not seem like I would be chosen for a teaching job anywhere. However, I trusted that God would provide for me to get this job, make more money and receive benefits. I had three interviews before the start of what would have been my third year as a teacher assistant, and I was hired at Green Run High School as a Special Education Teacher. I never went to my third interview because less than twenty-four hours after my interview, human resources called and offered me the job. God is truly amazing. Don't ever allow man's limitations to cause you to doubt the possible exceptions because God's favor is on your life.

Although I had taken the prerequisite classes to be a Special Education teacher, I would now be working as a full-time teacher and still going to school to get my master's degree in teaching with an emphasis in Special Education for the next three years. That sounds like a lot, doesn't it? Well, it absolutely was challenging. It was nobody but God and the support of the people around me to manage the weight of all that I was embarking on. Nevertheless, in August 2015, I was excited to be going through training to teach my own classes and begin my first year at Green Run High School.

As a new teacher, it was a combination of extreme excitement and nervousness, as with any new position that you step into. You present yourself confidently in that interview, but you are terrified when it is time to truly step into the new role. Nevertheless, I trusted God to be with me every step of the way. He did not fail me at all. I was eager to teach a new set of students with varying challenges to learn new material despite those challenges. As someone who believes that individuals can do better than people expect them to do, I took that into my classroom. I was ready to challenge these students based on where they were.

However, I was met with some pushback. This truly tested my character and strength in my first year. On top of working full time and being a full-time student, there were people that my approach to teaching was impractical for the population of students I taught. They never knew how difficult it was to be told by another teacher in the department that the people I had to work the closest with were talking about me to my department chair behind my back. It was absolutely devastating. There were days that the burden I carried trying to manage work, school, and opposition made me come home and cry. I felt isolated and alone at work, and I wondered if I would make it to the end of the school year. Nonetheless, I trusted God and would not forfeit my promise and blessing because it was hard.

When you did not have it easy growing up, you learn to be resilient at a young age. I remembered the days with the lights, water, and heat off, but those things never defined me. I remember being a child telling my mom she could not tell me I was poor because God was rich. I told my mom of my dreams of having a mansion, a butler, and a maid. I never really knew what profession would get me there, but I am still certain that my future looks that way. Faith and dreams always seem crazy until they become a reality. Looking back as an adult and understanding the economics and the poverty line, I understand by the world's definition that my family was "poor." Yes, I was the student on free, not reduced lunch. I was in the programs that took students on outings to the jail with hopes that we would avoid that future. However, God instilled something in my heart that could not be swayed. Since God was on the throne, I was not then and will never be poor. I learned that poverty is a mindset. If you settle into a certain mindset, then you can expect anything more.

The resilience that was birthed as a child showed up in my life as an adult. There I was, struggling to maintain my sanity, and God was with me every step of the way. I remember when a former pastor, Pastor Mark Lawrence, told a story about buying people at his job lunch and apologizing even though he did nothing wrong to "heap coals of fire on their heads" with kindness. That was just the story that shifted me from victimhood to a place of intentionality and faith.

Before the Christmas break of my first-year teaching, I brought lunch for the teachers who talked about me, and I apologized for teaching in a way they did not agree with. I explained that I was teaching the way I had been trained and the way I felt comfortable. When I came back from Christmas break, it was a completely different atmosphere at work. I knew I had passed the test. By the time I resigned as an educator, it was those same individuals who would stick up for me, encourage me, and we even laughed together. I allowed God to be glorified in that situation.

In my second year of teaching, I was shifted to work in classes with a mixture of both general education students and special education students who needed support but could learn and retain information in standard classes. This opened a completely different experience for me that I loved. I met more students and teachers than I did when I was teaching in a self-contained environment. I became the active person I had always been growing up in school. I became a cosponsor of the Young Life Program and participated in a student versus staff step-off and student versus staff basketball game. All my greatest memories of being an educator happened after my first year, which started off truly challenging. If I had allowed the opposition to make me quit, it would have stopped me from all the impact that I made in the future.

Being a Special Education teacher is a rewarding job as you help students overcome challenges academically, socially, and personally. You get to inspire and empower the next generation to be more than what society tries to limit them to be. I worked with a population of students that had similar stories that I had growing up, and I was honored to be a light in their lives, whether they were there for all four years with me or only for a short period.

As an educator in the school system, I was also able to connect with students outside of special education. I met amazing students like Hannah, Naya, AJ, Jake, East, and many more. I had no idea the impact that I could have on them, but it was also their impact on me. The beautiful thing about working with students is that there is joy and such a truly refreshing youthfulness. Although life is becoming more complicated for them, there are so many possibilities before them for their futures. I enjoyed motivating and encouraging young people to be leaders. I encouraged them to challenge the norm and be great. It can be scary to do the opposite of what society deems acceptable at times. Peer pressure is not always blatant, but it can also be unspoken pressure just to fit in. Through being involved in Young Life, the basketball program, the black history program, and many other things, I was able to reach the hearts of all types of students, and I truly enjoyed it.

Chapter 2
The struggle to Balance it All

In 2016, I went through a challenge in my personal life after only being a teacher for one year that really had me struggling mentally every day. It was a devastating blow that took place in my marriage. How do I focus on work with fear, hurt, and pain taking over my mind? How do I balance being present for students at a job I need to work and being okay myself?

In 2016, it was the birth of my ministry, and it would also be the starting place for a future business. My heart for God caused me to pull on the source of my help when I needed him the most. I have always been a private person, so I fought alone for a long time. However, this time God brought a great friend and spiritual parents into my life to help me navigate through the level of pain I was in. I was not as strong back then as I am today. Although, my strength was only realized because of the storms I encountered. What could have caused me to lose my mind in 2016 is what allowed me to give birth to greatness.

I am a living witness that pain will birth purpose. Out of all that I went through, pulling on God, I started a blog called New Beginnings with me. The blog did not evolve into anything incredible, but it was a yes to God. It was a yes to the understanding that I could not spend my life helping others and neglecting God's call on my life. A passion had been ignited for ministry. By 2017, I ended up writing two books. In 2018, I published another book, plus a book specifically for high school students.

What the enemy thought would be a setback actually pulled me further into purpose. The reality is that challenge will always show you what's in you. It will show you where your faith is also. From all the challenges that I have faced in my life, I can say that my life truly belongs to God. I could have turned away from God and lived a life beneath what he called me to out of pain, but God held me close.

The blog and books were live, including a Monday Motivation video. What I was doing outside of being a teacher became more exciting than what I was doing as a teacher. My love for being an example to young people never went away. The other components of the job requirements were no longer enjoyable to me. God pulled me into purpose, and I knew it was nothing I needed to let go of. He did not carry me through tragedy and trauma for me to go back to who I was before. He allowed something in me to rise again. The young girl growing up in a Pentecostal church who dreamed of being a missionary but was denied the opportunity by a leader that crushed her to the core was alive again. All the visions and possibilities of my future began to breathe again.

The call on my life did not require the validation of a man. When you walk through something with God, you let go of the need for someone to tell you it's okay to move. You set your eyes on him and choose to be obedient even when it makes you look crazy. I did so much that many people were not doing yet. It was not because I was so brave or confident all the time, but I kept choosing to be obedient to God, who has a purpose for my life.

In 2018, God put it in my heart to become a life coach. I did not have a lot of understanding of what it meant to be a life coach, but I said yes. I had no idea what that yes was bringing me into. I saw it as just another way of doing ministry, but it was really God shifting me into the realm of business. I truly had no idea of what I was walking into. After finishing my master's degree to become a teacher, I shifted into a doctorate program at Regent University to study Christian Leadership. So, when I had the option to choose which program I wanted to be certified in, it only made sense that leadership and life coaching were what they would be for me.

This shifted me into a new season of learning and exploration. I finally received my certificate of completion in 2019. It seemed like the tragedy of 2019 was long behind me, and the forward progression of my life was taking me down a path that I could be excited about. However, there was residue from experiences of 2016 that were still showing up even in 2019. What seemed like I had moved to the past was absolutely something that I dealt with, and my identity was flawed. The insecurity, the rejection, the abandonment, and the self-doubt still were a whisper in my ear.

Chapter 3
The Year I Found Me

Although all these things were being suppressed in my mind, I was still building, writing, and encouraging others. I was fighting the challenges of my mind because I was working to be better every day. I was determined to fulfill my purpose. I was in a relationship with God. However, there were deeply wounded areas that could no longer go unnoticed. There were areas in my life that required more attention. I was naive to think that things would just disappear or I would just randomly get better. It was immature for me to believe that I would eventually just be okay despite the nagging fears and paranoia that existed in my heart from 2019.

Was I phony? No. There was just another level of healing that I needed to go through with God. There was a layer of my heart that I had not truly handed over to God, and it would be in this next season that it was required.

In September 2019, I shut down. I stopped everything that I was doing. I stopped building, creating, and serving others and focused on myself. The challenges of my life were overwhelming. I had to deal with trauma from my past as a child, challenges in my present, and the fear of failure in my future.

I had so many hopes and dreams, it seemed like the life that I had was far from what I had hoped for. It was even far from what others even saw for me. What do you do when you look at your life and feel unsatisfied? What do you do when you look at your life and feel like what went wrong? What do you do when you look at your life and wonder if you made the wrong choice? What do you do when you look at your life and wonder if God led you here or if you got yourself here? Then the most famous question - God, why?

These were the questions I asked myself. I was trying to understand what was happening in my life. I felt defeated, alone, and without help. However, God met me at my rock bottom place. The place where I was literally tired of crying. I was tired of being angry and bitter. I was tired of being a person I did not want to be. I was tired to be the right person for everyone else and thinking that something was wrong with me.

I took time, and I asked God new hard questions. God, what is my purpose? God, I know I am doing this, and I am doing that. However, God, I will stop everything if this is not what you have for me. God, show me where you want me and what you want me to do. From September to December was a reformation of my life. My one-on-one time with God was everything. I took trips to Starbucks, Panera, Barnes and Nobel to read and study. I dealt with my heart. I processed my pain. I allowed myself to cry. I told God I would not hold on to anything nor define myself by a role I held in anyone's life. It was no longer most important to be a wife, daughter, sister, leader, intercessor, influencer, author, or coach, but it was about being enough as his daughter.

In those few months, God took me to a serious level of inner healing and maturation. It was the beginning of a journey I chose to be forever on with him. Real Talk Kim's live at 9 pm helped save my life. Every night she would be on, saying, "Get up." She said, "When you hit rock bottom, you find out who the rock is at the bottom." I came to terms with 2019 being my rock bottom year. I had a choice to make - would I get up with God or give up and die? Not necessarily a natural death but a spiritual death.

In December 2019, a new woman rose from the ashes. It was not that life had become perfect, but it was because I had gained a new perspective from time with God. I had gained the clarity that I needed. God had secured my identity in being his daughter, and I understood that no matter how much I wanted life to go a certain way, God's will was best for me. These words are easy to say but harder to live. However, a yes to God is the best decision we will ever make.

I started sharing my story. I told myself about the mask, the molestation, the marital challenges, and the fear of failure. Then, I went from doing Monday Motivation videos all by myself to interviewing other women. God had done a work in me that perfection was no longer needed. Either I would be loved for my whole story or not. I would no longer try to be what other people wanted me to be. I would instead be who I was authentically and unapologetically.

I finished 2019 with a bang. I wrote a book in thirty days, created a planner, and developed my first program as a coach called Overcoming in 2020. I had many people who signed up; I was thankful and eager to take on the new, although I had no idea what was up ahead.

Chapter 4
Unexpected Pain and Heartache

As you can tell, I had very high hopes for 2020. I was in great expectation because of what God had brought me out of. The clarity I received in 2019 and the processing that I went through prepared me for what was next. I was sure of it. This was the year that I planned to allow my coaching business to go to the next level. I had created a group coaching program called Overcome in 2020, and all that shifted at the end of 2019. I was eager to begin a journey of leading again from a whole place. The people who signed up with me not only were with me for the month of January, but some of them even decided to keep me on for coaching.

However, something tragic happened on January 26, 2020. Kobe Bryant, his daughter, and others died tragically in a car accident. I have never cried over the passing of a celebrity before, but the news of Kobe passing literally crushed me. My first ever book report in middle school was Kobe Bryant. My only basketball jersey as a kid was Kobe Bryant. I watched him growing up, and I cheered him on in my adulthood, winning championship after championship against all the odds. He became a voice of change, inspiration, and motivation as I heard him speak about his mentality for winning. He is a legend. I struggled trying to wrap my mind around his loss. It is always hard when someone dies, but it is even more devastating when they die young. My heart went out to his wife and his family to lose not just him but also his beautiful daughter. My sister-in-law told my husband and me in a text group that Kobe died, which is very ironic, and you will see how later as you keep reading this chapter.

After the loss of Kobe, I thought that surely that would be the most devastating loss I would experience that year. The way my heart ached at the news, I did not need anything else, nor did the world, in my opinion.

Mr. #10 is gone, but I don't understand why

On March 2, 2020, another devastating loss hit my life and many others I knew. This loss was not worldwide, but the state of Virginia felt it, especially the Hampton roads area. With respect to the family, I'll say Mr. #10. Mr. #10 graduated from school the previous year and was a basketball team member. Mr. #10 was a leader, a great kid, and a young man with so much potential. As I taught book club and young life, he was one of the students that stood out. He was a young man full of joy and confidence, ready to take on the world. Mr. #10 was respectful and always the life of any space he was in. I remember in his young life, he was never afraid of dance competitions, games competitions, or singing competitions. He would lead the other basketball team members to participate. His energy was infectious. I even remember one day I went to do book club for the basketball team in his senior year; as I was coming in, he said, "Hold on Mrs. Thomas." As a leader, he had a conversation with his team challenging them to push and do better to win. It was a proud teacher moment. It was that type of leadership in a student you dreamed of seeing.

This tall, athletic, and fun-loving kid went on and played the next level of basketball. He took a year in a program that would prepare him for college basketball. He decided that he felt it was best for him to sharpen his skills and position himself for greater success. His confidence made you believe that his choice was the best. I always told him that wherever he went, my husband and I would come to see him play.

My husband was given this opportunity to perform his music at a military academy. On the day of the event, we had no idea what to expect. As I was setting up the camera for my husband to be able to stream his video live, I heard a voice behind me say, "Mrs. Thomas." I thought to myself, *No one knows me here.* I turned around with great curiosity, and to my surprise was that fun-loving kid I knew from work but with a haircut now. He was standing up tall, confident, and with a big smile. He came and gave me a big hug, and I greeted him.

He rushed to the stage to join my husband because he already knew all his songs. In his senior year, my husband was a volunteer basketball coach, and he had one-on-one sessions with some of the players and gave them a ride back home, and Mr. #10 always made sure to get a ride with my husband. My husband played his music on the rides and had talks about basketball and so many other things. Mr. #10, being the leader he was, not only went up there, but he also brought other students with him. The life of the party showed that it was cool to enjoy the high energy performance my husband was giving. He was still that amazing kid everyone loved. Later that day, he had a game, and we went to see him play.

We came back to Virginia, and I was so excited to share that I had seen Mr. #10. I grabbed pictures of him playing in a game, and I again felt like a proud teacher. Who knew that would be the last time

I saw him play basketball and cheer for him as loud as possible? The boys' basketball team had a game at the Norfolk Scope to go on to regionals again. The year prior, Mr. #10 had a buzzer-beater there that had the world going crazy, which took them to regionals, but they did not become champions that year. Mr. #10 was there to support his former team and celebrate them. I wondered that night how he felt, but I knew he was excited for them. I did not get to hug him that day as I was leaving. I did not want to embarrass him by talking with his friends, but I sure wish I did.

I came into work the next day looking to celebrate even more, but I was greeted by a teacher I worked with telling me the horrific news that Mr. #10 died later that night. My body became lifeless as I dropped to the ground in agony. God, how is this possible? Why Mr. #10? I was screaming and crying. I had no words. What was happening? Was this real? How could this be? I could hear people talking around me, but I could not comprehend. I could not stop crying. I could not get up from the floor. I could hear them calling my husband to come back and get me, but I still could not get off the floor and stop myself from crying. A student I had come to see so much promise and potential in was gone. It seemed like what people say - gone too soon.

That day, I cried even more at home; days and days later, I cried. Walking through the halls, I cried, and I was afraid to see the basketball team again. I did not have words to say anything. One day in the hallway, I saw the coach and some of the boys were with him; they circled me just to say everything was going to be okay. I needed their strength. I know they needed mine too. I took a break from the book club and came back for one final lesson with them. It was the hardest lesson I have ever had to teach to inspire and encourage the hearts of young people that I was sure had some of the same questions that I had. God gave me strength. The boys went on to be champions that year. After all of that, surely something better was going to come, right?

Well, on March 13, 2020, the school shut down because we found ourselves in a worldwide pandemic. We were told we had to stay in our homes because people got this new virus and died. I call 2020 the year of crying. It was a year full of mourning in our world. We were trying to navigate a hard season. I was trying to wrap my mind around the pain of all that happened and keep obeying God with the things he was calling me to do. In the midst of a pandemic and pain, I was giving birth to purpose. I shifted and started calling, interviewing people on the Power and Grace Leaders Talk Show. When school was closed, I interviewed women on Monday, Wednesday, and Friday about their stories.

The journey of purpose that I was on began to accelerate during the pandemic. I received a scholarship to be a part of the Next Level Business Academy with Dr. Dean, and I was trained on how to launch a program that would be even more impactful to the people God called me to reach. I was building; I have learned that pain will either cause you to crumble or you will rise and win. I was pushing. We don't know when our time will be. This was more real with the reality of everything that was happening.

You would think that pushing beyond that pain would be just a continuation of a joyful victory after the devastation of these things. However, these two losses together did not compare to the loss on Mother's Day of 2020. The loss left me speechless.

Not My Sister-In-Law Jesus!

Mother's Day is normally a hard day for me because of fertility challenges. 2020 was the first Mother's Day after dealing with the shame of my story in 2019 that I shared my heart about how this day can be difficult for women like me. It was also the day I was sure to say Happy Mother's Day to my mom, sister-in-law, and mother-in-law without an aching pain in my heart. It was the first Mother's Day I felt pretty good since being married.

We went to visit a friend's house that day, and we stopped and purchased food from WaWa on the way back home. My husband and I walked in through the garage door of our one-bedroom apartment. The kitchen was on the right, our full bath on the left, and in front of us was our black futon. My husband's phone rang. He picked up the phone with the food bag in the other hand. Suddenly, there was a terror that set in his eyes and an expression on his face I could never forget. He said, "Wait, what?" I was asking, "What was going on?" He was saying, "Mom, what?" I kept asking what was going on. He replied, "My mom just said Lexus is dead." I walked backward. I screamed, "God tell me this is not true. God, there is no way. God, what is going on?" My mind was racing, and I was trying to figure out what to do and say. What is my husband telling me? What is my husband about to do? He got off the phone and walked in circles. He kicked the futon and left the house.

There I was in the house by myself. I was praying, trying to wrap my mind around the news. I didn't drop to the floor. God gave me some crazy strength that I can only see in hindsight. I called my friend Kiyanni and told her what was going on. She and Justin were already on their way before my husband came back into the house, and we cried together. There was a rage in his eyes. Our friends came over, and there was an utter shock going through my system. What words do you say? What do you do? What happens when you are a believer and tragedy strikes? When you have prayed for your loved ones and in a moment, they are gone. Her abusive ex-boyfriend was driving the car in a single-car accident where only her life was lost.

I can't go into any more details of all that transpired and the level of pain I endured. My husband still cries for losing his little sister. I had known her since she was fourteen, but he had known her all her life. I could never fathom the level of pain he felt in his heart. All I could do was pray and console him when he allowed me. There were no words or scripture that I could say to him that would erase or ease his pain.

This was the final devastating blow of 2020. In this one-bedroom, a part where the pandemic caused us to remain, all of this loss had been remembered. Nevertheless, I pushed forward. The only answer I have is to rely on God. The reset of 2019 was not just preparing me for blessings, but it was also preparing me for pain. The roots that went deeper into God in 2019 held me up in 2020.

PART II
He Knows Best

FROM PAIN TO PURPOSE

CHAVON ANETTE

Chapter 5
God, I say Yes

After 2019, my life truly started shifting for the better pertaining to business and ministry. Although 2020 had been filled with so much loss and tears, things were also working in my favor as I stepped out in faith and obeyed God during so much turmoil. A few defining moments happened in 2020 that set me on a new course for my life that has been far greater than I could have ever imagined. As believers, we must understand that we can miss out on God's best plan for our lives without a yes. The fullness of our lives is outside of our comfort zone, our normal, and even our current circle.

Marketing Mogul- Dr. Shameika Dean

The first defining moment in 2020, amid hosting the Power & Grace Leaders talk show, I met so many amazing women who were doing incredible things on earth. However, the first woman I will talk about that has been pivotal to my business shifting to the next level is Dr. Shameika Dean. I had been following Dr. Dean for a while. Honestly, when I asked her to be a part of the show, I was afraid to ask, but I was being obedient to God. Dr. Dean is a well-established businesswoman and also a woman of faith. Those two things are what make me admire her. She is a woman who stands tall as a marketing mogul but also one who gives language to what it takes to be successful as an entrepreneur without compromising who you are as a person of faith.

Dr. Dean was completely open to allowing me to interview her, and I was in total shock. It's funny because how I felt about Dr. Dean is how people sometimes see me - unreachable because of the high regard for her work. However, talking with her, she is absolutely down to earth and truly passionate about serving people in a way that allows them to destroy old mindsets and step into the fullness of their potential as business owners.

During the interview, I was both nervous and excited. She was more phenomenal than I imagined as she shared her story from a transparent and vulnerable place and why she helps people reach a place of wealth in their businesses for the strength of the family unit. Dr. Dean is one of those individuals who are bold, confident, and masterful in the area that she leads on the earth as a speaker, content creator, course creator, and marketing mogul. As I listened to her words, I knew that I had to be connected to what she was doing next. I had already come to terms with myself that I would be willing to invest in myself as a business owner. For years, I supported my husband in the things he was building, and it was time to really give my all to what God had called me to do. It was time for me to invest in what God placed in me. John Maxwell said if you want to do something small, do it alone, but if you want to do something big, do it with a team. If you really want God to exceed your expectations, invest in the people he puts in your path that have language for your purpose.

I bought myself and my cousin, Shelia, a ticket to her course launch called "The Launch of the Next Level Business Academy." I was excited about this three-day event. I participated, and I was fully present to learn all I could and get ready to sign up for what was next. Dr. Dean mentioned that someone would receive a scholarship also. There was no guarantee that it would be me, but whether I was the recipient or not, I believed God that I would be able to get whatever funds to be a part of the New Level Business Academy. As a family, Dr. Dean and her family hosted these amazing days. It was big, she looked beautiful, her daughter was an amazing host, her husband helped with set up and camera work, and her son performed his music and showcased his clothing line. When I tell you this launch was extraordinary, it is an understatement.

On the final day, Dr. Dean announced space for people to sign up, and there would be time to sign up later as well, but with a deadline. I had a plan to sign up later. I had faith that God would provide for me. Remember, I was just really walking into the entrepreneurial sector in 2020 with the launch of the Overcoming in 2020 course as a coach. Although I still had coaching clients, I was not well established financially as a business owner, and I was living on a teacher's salary. Nonetheless, I knew God had connected me with Dr. Dean for a reason, and he was going to ensure that I was a part of her exploits because I needed training and education as a new business owner.

As Dr. Dean was about to announce the scholarship recipient, I said, "God, if you allow me to win this scholarship, this will be my sign that I am exactly where you want me to be despite everything that has happened in my life." Dr. Dean said, "The scholarship winner is… CHAVON THOMAS." "LOOK!!!" I screamed, jumped, cried, shouted, and ran around the house! My husband sitting and playing the Xbox, looked back at me and said, "What happened?" I replied, "I JUST WON

THE SCHOLARSHIP! GOD DID IT! I KNOW THIS IS WHAT I'M SUPPOSED TO BE DOING!" Then, I came back to the computer and tried to use my fingers to type the level of excitement.

Next, it was on me to make every moment of my time with Dr. Dean count. I worked diligently. I participated in group discussions and video meetings. I did every assignment that challenged my limited thinking, prepared me for the development of a new and more developed course, and allowed me to strengthen my story to reach the people I was called to. In November, I launched, The Fire Academy. The price was higher, and many people signed up. It was a one-year program. As each person signed up, I found myself filled with so much joy. Lives were about to be transformed as I poured into others everything that I had come to learn in stepping out as an entrepreneur with God.

My life shifted, and I no longer see myself as one who does great things from a ministry perspective, but I had the ability to do great things for the glory of God in both the marketplace and ministry. I believe in this season that God is breathing on his people to step into the realm of business and soar without compromise. I had never dreamed of being a business owner, but I knew I would write a book and travel the world preaching the gospel because those were things God showed me and were prophesized over my life.

I took the limitations off of my future, and I allowed God to stir the ship of my life, and he has exceeded my expectations with a new act of obedience. I believe God is looking for representatives to reach every mountain of influence, and if we say that ministry is the only avenue he can do that; we miss the magnitude of his wisdom and power through his body.

The Confidence Queen- Destiny Inspire

The second defining moment was connecting with Destiny Inspire. She was also another person in 2020 that God brought into my life. When you have faced certain obstacles that cause you to challenge your value and your worth as a woman, confidence is one of those things that will rob you of your purpose.

When I was 12 years old, God told me that being a teacher was what he called me to do, and I desired to answer the call, which I absolutely did. As an adult, I spoke at many events, but the level at which my paradigm shifted had everything to do with my confidence internally that I could truly travel the world as a speaker for both ministry and the marketplace. Comparison, imposture syndrome, fear of failure, and fear of rejection were the things that were holding me back as a speaker.

Destiny Inspire was another person that I interviewed on the Power & Grace Leaders talk show. She announced after her amazing interview, where she said no more shrinking back, that she was hosting a conference called Killer Confidence. I knew when I interviewed her that I needed to be there. I invested in Killer Confidence, and it was life-changing. After that conference, she opened the launch of Sis, Speak Up. It was a four-week intensive helping people craft their stories and become impactful speakers. That grabbed my attention. As a speaker, I don't want to just be empowering and inspiring, but I want what is said to be something people will remember and experience transformation. So, I invested in the program. I invested for the first time in what I had been doing since I was a kid.

John Maxwell says that it's important to focus on making the things that are your strengths even stronger. In my studying as a leader, I have learned about the power of operating in your zone of genius. Your zone of genius is what you are innately good at, and it is what fulfills you when you do it. This sounds good, right? But so many people flow in the zone of incompetence, competence, and excellence, but they fail to ensure they are flowing in their zone of genius. For me, coaching, speaking, teaching, and writing are my zones of genius. These things excite me, and if I could do them every day, I would without pay. Just because I could do them without pay and feel great does not mean that I should. I have learned personally that what I have to offer, share, impart, and teach is worth investing in. If you are reading this and have struggled with charging for what you do, ask yourself why you feel like you are not worth someone investing in you for your time, experience, and expertise? That is an old way of thinking, and it must be removed for you to excel further into purpose.

In Sis, Speak Up, I gained confidence, strategy, and a larger sisterhood. I was challenged in week four not to be afraid to present myself to the world, so I executed. I showed up with even more confidence and fire. In all that was happening in 2020, God gave me my name. The Fire Leadership Coach. He said, "Chavon, you are now a woman of Fire." Between Dr. Dean and Coach Destiny, I allowed God to do a completely new work in my heart and mind. I was and still am unstoppable for the glory and honor of God, which also led to the development of my signature course program, formerly known as "She's on Fire Academy" and now "The Fire Academy" for all kingdom people. I am not the person I was before 2019, even with all the great things I did before that rock bottom year.

December 2020 was crazy.

The third defining moment of my life happened in December 2020. This was the month God did two amazing things in my life.

First, I became an Amazon #1 Bestselling author sharing my story of becoming an educator. It was interesting because I knew God was calling me off my job, and he would do it soon. I did not have a date in mind, but I knew the struggle of balancing all the things that I was doing and being a teacher with the increasing demands during a pandemic was becoming overwhelming at the rate of the acceleration that was happening in my life. My passion for business and ministry had increased drastically. The stress of being a teacher in the public education system no longer seemed like something I wanted to carry. I absolutely loved impacting students' lives through lessons, talks, motivation, and empowerment, but the workload that came along with it was becoming more strenuous than joyous for me. I concluded later that teaching was my zone of excellence, but it was not my zone of genius. There were elements of being an educator that allowed me to tap into my zone of genius, but there were other things that just drained me.

As a new Amazon #1 Bestselling author, it opened opportunities for me. At the start of 2021, I spoke on the news and a TV network, sharing my story. It was amazing, and I was not afraid to put myself out there because Sis, Speak Up says, "Confidently present yourself." I cried those days as I spoke to the world not as a minister but as a marketplace leader. Everything that had been put in place in 2020 was showing tangible results. I knew God was with me. I knew God had called me to ministry.

The second big moment in December happened on December 22, 2020. I had become acquainted with clubhouse through Destiny Inspire.

After our four-week intensive ended in November, she sent me an invite to clubhouse and invited another classmate; they invited another until we were all connected. Clubhouse was a powerful tool to network with people around the world. Since my business started taking off during the pandemic, I had not gotten connected with many business owners because the world was shut down. Clubhouse was a great place for people to connect, but I have connected with Christian entrepreneurs, and leaders around were doing amazing things. It was beautiful to see a world where there were so many people pursuing the same purpose as me. My conferences, talk shows, and podcast are all international because of the people I connected with around the world online. It was beautiful watching everything unfold. It was in a clubhouse room where I asked about taking the leap of faith and leaving my job, and they told me it is a matter of faith to take the leap. It was memorable because I really came to a true understanding that fear was holding me back.

On one of the late nights in December, I was at clubhouse, and Apostle John Eckhart was hosting a room. If you know who he is, you know the room was both powerful and insightful. He allowed people to raise their hands to come on the stage and allow some of him and his constituents to flow prophetically. With hundreds of people in the room, I did not expect to be chosen to come on stage. When they invited me on the stage, I felt like I would have a heart attack. I said, "I can't believe they called me up!" Prophet Jon Michael prophesied over me, and what he said brought comfort, edification, exhortation, and clarity. I cried and cried that night as he ministered to me through God's revelation, wisdom, and power. One huge thing that he said that I kept running away from for years was that I was called to be a prophet and that the word of knowledge was strong in my life. I told God. "These people know nothing about me. If they have confirmed what's in my life, then

I can no longer run. I accept the prophetic mantle upon my life." I cried and cried. This 'yes' was the one God had been waiting for years for me to say. I have said yes to business and ministry, but it was this mantle in my life that I kept disqualifying myself from. My life changed for the better in 2021 because of that yes.

In this season, be encouraged to say yes to God even in the scary things. I know there were times when running away from the call seemed easier. However, as long as God has called you, it's only a matter of time before you completely surrender. He is a patient God who will continue to pull on you and put people in your path until you answer the call.

Chapter 6
The Valley of Decisions

January 2021 began the ride of my life as it pertained to God, truly blowing my mind. I began the 2021 Inner Circle Retreat. The theme was Acceleration. My word for this year was 'reward.' God told me that he was about to bring me into a season of reward for all things I had been encountering in my life. The entire first quarter of 2021 was phenomenal. I was being stretched with my new mantle in clubhouse, and I was leading the First Academy and coaching new clients. Then in February 2021, I was interviewed on the news, a speaker at the school where I obtained my undergraduate degree (Virginia Wesleyan University), and interviewed on a talk show that hundreds of thousands of people tuned in to watch. By this time, I was really seeing God's hand in my life, and the decision of whether or not I would leave my job was the pressing question over my head.

Was I really ready to leave the job I went to get my master's degree to obtain? Was I really going to leave the comfort of work that guaranteed a check semi-monthly and trust God in the realm of entrepreneurship? I had been nominated for teacher of the year that year. I felt like God allowed them to recognize me for the time that I was there. I had made an impact there, and it could not be denied. I was confused about the nomination, but I was also thankful. God is amazing that way in that he would allow me to be recognized for my time at the school. I loved it for the time I was called to be there.

I tossed and turned all night, and I had conversations with my husband about it. I asked him how he felt about me leaving my job. He did not object. I told him when I felt like it was about to happen sooner than I thought. My heart was to wait until the end of the year to resign. However, I felt God telling me sooner. One day at home, I wrote my resignation letter. After a meeting with my Principal and Assistant Principal about how I felt trying to manage the demands of being an educator this season, I was asked a question about my passion. I knew where my passion was now, and it was not with being an educator. That day, I turned in my resignation letter.

I went home, and I sat in front of my TV and cried. I said, "God, I did it. I am being obedient to take this leap with you. God, I am trusting you to provide everything that I need." I felt his peace, and as the days went forth in March, I nicely trained the new teacher who would be replacing me. I greeted everyone who asked me questions with kindness, but I knew it was my time to go. I had hard conversations with students, but it was time for a big shift. Although it was uncomfortable for others, their discomfort was not more severe than mine.

In March, I went to a conference called the Go-Getter Conference by Candace, and there was an opportunity for grants. All we had to do was sign up for a program and submit a video sharing our story of why we should be grant recipients. I talked about the new leap I was taking, and I shared that I needed my own laptop because I was an online-based businessperson. On March 13, 2021, on my ninth anniversary, I was at a conference learning and staying connected to find out if I had won one of the grants. My husband was frustrated, but I said I would be ready for our movie date in time. That night before the movies, I was thrilled to hear the announcement that I was the $500 grant winner to buy a laptop. My husband and I went out to the movies, but he was not very happy with me. If I went back in time, would I make a different choice? The answer is no. I love my husband; however, I was taking the biggest leap of faith of my life, and I needed something that we did not have - knowledge for this new season and money to buy a new laptop because any money coming in was going to bills.

Furthermore, the challenges that we had been experiencing together would not get erased in one night. So I jumped and shouted at the news of being a grant winner and then went to the movies to celebrate my anniversary. It would have been nice to really celebrate together being a grant winner, but I was fine thanking God for what he did for me. It is this same laptop I developed more programs and courses, went live, wrote more books (including this), met with coaching clients, instructed people to become coaches, and impacted more lives after my leap than I thought possible in one year.

PART III
The Journey Filled with Miracles

FROM PAIN TO PURPOSE

CHAVON ANETTE

Chapter 7
Walking by Faith

Walking by faith looked like the greatest leap of my life. I am not sure of everyone else's story, but my story looks like this: a smart black girl from Virginia goes to college, gets a degree and works to become a doctor or a lawyer. On the journey desiring to fit that mold, I pursued education instead and became a Special Education teacher provisional license. It was still an honorable job. There was a steady income. I got my master's degree in teaching, which allowed me to obtain my official license after passing the tests required on the first try - thank God. When it is required that you must invest in tests, pray that the first try you pass because no one wants to keep spending money. I had done what was expected of me; however, God had another plan for my life.

I stepped into a realm of entrepreneurship, and God was calling me forward. In prayer, God told me once that my call was to lead, and later, he shared with me that I was the Fire Leadership Coach. Then, he helped me understand that I would go as the coach even when I went to minister. I was not a coach because it was cool but because God called me to this work on earth.

Finally, on April 2nd, 2021, I took the biggest leap of my life. I walked away from my job of being an educator with just six years of experience. My parents were shocked, and many people were too. I did not leave because my business was booming. I was making money with my business, making more than I ever had; however, I left because God said it was time. I could turn in the school laptop, say goodbye to the coworkers and students I loved, and walk away with my head held high as I took this new journey with God. I had faith in what God was getting ready to do in my life. My theme scripture since 2020 has been Ephesian 3:20, "Now until him who is able to do exceeding abundantly above all we can ask or think according to the power that works within us." This was the season to believe in God. This was the season to trust God with my life. This was the season to be completely surrendered to a path that seemed uncommon, but it was a path he called me into. It could seem crazy, but faith looks crazy until the evidence of your faith is materialized. The person with the faith is standing and living on a word that no one else is responsible for but themselves. We must be obedient to God.

However, although I had taken this big leap, and the pressure was off my back from working as an educator, and I could just focus on business and ministry, I was still fighting. At home, although my husband said he supported my decision, the reality was that during the pandemic, all the challenges in my marriage went from bad to worse. He was navigating through the loss of his sister, and I tried my best to be there for him as much as he would allow me, but you can only help someone as far as they allow you. What happens when the greatest war you fight is the war inside your home? The place where you want to feel the most secure and safe is the very place of your greatest pain. I was celebrating the biggest leap while fighting my greatest war. Days in the house for hours by myself, but I'm working and building. I'm praying and believing God for a change in my business and my home. All this acceleration was happening, yet all of this warfare was too as I tried to process purpose and pain. You never know where your battle will be in this life, and the enemy targets what will hurt you the most.

Still, I pressed forward because I believed things would get better. For years, what I held on to my shoulders was relieved. There were many sleepless nights. There were many nights and days filled with tears, but I knew God would see me through it all. Many people had no idea about the war I was in; that's why you should not be envious of someone's success because you never know the cost of their journey or even the cost of their anointing. My anointing was birthed out of pain because it caused me to pull on God more. My pain made me look to God more. I heard someone say the challenges sharpen your ear to his voice. I believe that 100%.

In the midst of all of that, I traveled for the first time out of state, where everything was taken care of, to go and speak as Prophetess Chavon Thomas. I was traveling to Texas, and I was going by myself. I did the most traveling with my ministry in 2021, but I traveled alone. It was exciting in one regard to travel and do what God showed me as a young girl, and I even shared with my husband the year I met him when we were dating. Looking up in the sky one night on the beach, I shared that I believed God would take me around the world preaching the gospel back in 2009. Now, here it was in 2021; God was beginning to expand my territory. Although I had been married and supporting my husband for years, I was seemingly taking this journey forward by myself. The thoughts of what was happening, while I was away, were disturbing, but I had an assignment. My life and purpose could not be put on hold because of fear and things I did not have control over, even if I tried.

I traveled to Texas, and God met us at that conference in a powerful way. God allowed me to preach with fire and boldness. I ministered prophetically as well. I was given space on Saturday that allowed me to minister freely. The people were blessed, and inner healing took place. As people say, I understood the assignment, but it was all God. God gives us the words to preach, which will be just what the people of God need. It can be terrifying going into a place you are not familiar with for the first time. Will you be received? I can honestly say there have been many who have received me, and I am thankful.

As I built my business and did ministry, I started working ten hours a week at Regent University in May. These ten hours a week took care of my car payment, and the business would take care of any other bills that needed to be covered. I also pulled my 401K, which was very helpful in the transition. Some would think maybe that was not a good idea, but I don't believe a 401K is what will sustain me in my future. It will be what God allows me to accomplish that is much more than what a 401K could ever do.

I trusted God to be Jehovah Jireh, the Lord who provides for himself. As God's daughter, faith meant to trust God beyond what I could see. I remember for a little while, my mom would send me to places that were hiring because that's all my parents really knew. I had to have a heart to heart with my mom to get her to understand that she did not need to do that. She completely understood. What was beautiful was that shifting into entrepreneurship shifted my life to allow me to be there for my mom more. There were seasons that I often needed her support, but I was able to bless her in this new season.

May was when I also birthed Powerhouse Leaders University. It is a place where Kingdom business owners or future business owners to-be, sign up for a safe paced course that I created. My sister Melissa Daughtry would come and do my makeup, and I would create new content with a beautifully "beat" face. I had no idea that this space would also house what God would allow me to walk into in the future, which was instructing people to become coaches. It would allow for a shift and a turn in my business. God opened up other doors as I helped others become Christian coaches to change the world.

Chapter 8
The writing on the Wall

In the midst of all that was happening in 2021, another life-changing prophetic word hit my life in August of that year. There was a guest at my church while my pastors were on a temporary sabbatical to focus on their families, which I believe was absolutely needed. Prophet T. Solomon came to our church as one of the guest speakers. Remember, amid all the great things God is having me do - build a business, travel the world and speak - there is a private battle I am fighting that only a handful of people are aware of. There are days when my husband is home, and there are days he is finding somewhere else to stay. It is an understatement when I say I am pressing toward the mark. I prayed and asked God for the month of August that he would allow someone who knew nothing about my story or my history to speak a word into my life. There is nothing wrong with making your request known to God even when you have people encouraging you and when you hear God for yourself.

There was a particular Sunday that I almost did not go to church, but I moved beyond my feelings and said I would go. The week before, I had to leave service early to pick up my husband from work because we only had one car. I was upset because I was afraid that I would miss the opportunity for God to answer my prayer and that he would be the reason. However, this Sunday, I almost didn't go. God had Prophet Solomon release a word to me. It was right after I had spoken a Saturday before at an event for one of my former clients remembering her daughter who passed away from traumatic brain injury and had a conversation with my leaders over the phone to make sure I still had their covering as I was doing so much ministry, which I did. That Sunday, God honored my prayer request. In the middle of Prophet Solomon's sermon, he stopped and released the word of the Lord over me. I was in complete shock, honestly. For me, once the sermon starts, the prophetic flow is typically released at the end of the sermon.

Prophet Solomon's word blessed my life beyond what he could have imagined. I will highlight a few things that blessed me that give you all a glimpse into how it spoke directly to me, which you can gather from reading the book up to this point. He called me "lady in the pink." The man of God had no idea who I was, but God knows us completely.

1. He said there is a long list of things you have been asking from God, and some I prayed for years ago and stopped because I did not see it yet. He said I was coming out of seven years of silence. One big thing he spoke about was wanting a child and a strong marriage. I had been married for nine years, and although there have been many prophecies, my baby had not come yet. I had not seriously brought that to God in a long time because of the excruciating pain it was causing me.

2. He said the Lord had been stretching me. It has been hard, ugly, uncomfortable, and not seem necessary. He was stretching me to prepare me for a new season. He said God had hidden me, and he was incubating what he had placed inside me. What

people don't understand is that what God has shown me he was going to do in my life is so much bigger than what I do today. In my challenges, he has been hiding and allowing me to position myself to hear his voice over the voices of others. All the pain I was fighting through drew me closer to the father.

3. He said if you would get over the hurt of men and women who did not understand you and forgive them, I will make you a sign and a wonder in your city. This was big because my greatest fight was at home. In all that had gone on in this new season, there were others who hurt me and betrayed me with their actions and words. I had to choose forgiveness for my purpose. I had to go back to praying for the things that I had not seen God do yet.

These are just three points from all that he released to me. There is so much more like the new anointing of dreams, prophetic power, and revelation that was coming on me. God answered my prayer, and it was just what I needed to continue forward in the year.

In September, I went on to host my first in-person workshop called Fanning the Flame Experience. It is now an annual workshop, and 2021 made it year number two. The previous one was virtual, just like Powerhouse Leaders Conference had to be virtual in 2020.

God met us in a powerful way at this conference. I preached, prophesied, and prayed with another level of power. Even on the second day of my workshop, there was a fight. However, my sisters poured into me before I ministered in a great and powerful way. To hear more about that, you would need to grab your copy of My Sister Helped Me Heal Vol. 1. available on all platforms.

God was truly doing something new in my life despite the challenges I was facing. In addition to that one challenge, the problem came in my health. My face would go numb on the left side. It started around June. I believe it was birthed through the stress I was under, and it was also an attack from the enemy. My other physical challenges are not as obvious. Not being able to have children is an internal physical matter, but my face shutting down to the point that my left eye closes and the left side of my mouth droops, this was terrifying. I prayed and cried, and I even received prayer for it. However, the problem persisted. It felt like a thorn in my flesh. I stopped going live as frequently because it was embarrassing. When I finally went to the hospital later, they ruled out lesions on the brain and strokes, but there were still more questions than answers.

However, I pressed forward. Nothing was going to stop my new yes in this season. All the things that I was up against would not stop me. That must be our mindset when it comes to purpose. The reality is that during the overflow of blessings, there are still obstacles. It is not a sign to stop or give up. Keep your eyes fixed on God and pursue.

Chapter 9
Purpose, Pain, Promise

In October, I had the beautiful honor to travel back to Texas for another speaking engagement. This was amazing because it gave me the opportunity to speak at my first in-person revival. As a young girl growing up in church, revivals were always a big deal. The opportunity to deliver a message to the people with the intention of reviving was mind-blowing. It was an absolute honor. I was completely humbled by it. However, while away, it was official that my husband had moved out of the house.

Here I was getting ready to speak at one of the most memorable moments of my life, and I was again traveling by myself. It was the reality that I was living with as I went forth in ministry. I was waiting for money to be released to me for months now that had not come yet. I was praying and believing God that at the right time, he would do it. I had bills to pay, and I had to do it myself. I had not let my parents know what was happening in my home because my responsibility is to protect my marriage even if things are shaky because I love my husband. My desire is for things to work out, and my family is absolutely biased toward me, which they should be. The reality of separation is alive and well, but my faith is still in God. My thought was that it would just be for a little while, and God would bring us back together. Nevertheless, it was all out of my control, so I continued to press forward. When the enemy is throwing you curve balls, you have to ask yourself, "Do I still believe that I can knock the ball out of the park with God on my side?"

The revival was powerful. Just like God did in Texas in April, he worked powerfully through me in October. I flowed prophetically. As I was closing my ministering, God had a sister that I connected with in April to support me and minister to me before she left. She released a word over me, and she said, "The money you have been waiting for would be released by the time you get back home." I cried and wept, and I believed God. She left, and I continued to minister to the last few people left at the altar. My friend recharged me at that moment, and God gave me a second wind to continue ministering.

I came back home with expectations, but I returned home on a Sunday. The money would be coming as a direct deposit, so I was waiting. On that Tuesday I anticipated, God being ever faithful, over $10,000 was released to my account. It was the money I had been waiting for. I did all the things I planned to do with that money. I paid my tithes; I paid my rent for the remainder of the year; I got a new car because my old car was beaten up, which was my fault; and I took care of other bills. I spent the money wisely. I cried, shouted and praised God because I did not have to ask my parents for money. God was taking care of me, and he still does. God can't fail us. God was blessing me abundantly beyond my wildest imagination.

In October, I launched out and began instructing people to become coaches. When I tell you I loved every moment of it, you still cannot understand the joy I get training people to become coaches. Not only did I start instructing people to become coaches, but he also allowed the creator of CLS Reflection Academy to ask me to become the COO of the company and Governing Accreditation Council. God was blowing my mind. I was helping people step further into purpose. I know I am called to be a leader to leaders, and my assignment is to help God's people rise. Through coaching, mentoring, course creation, speaking, writing, and so much more, God has allowed me to do just that.

As I closed out the year in December, it was the second annual Powerhouse Leaders Conference. It was a hybrid conference, and when I tell you it was grand and powerful, it is truly an understatement; there were speakers, panel guests, dancers, and more. The cherry on top was that Coach Destiny inspired being one of my headline speakers. That was another investment that I made with the money released in October. I prayed about God providing me with what I needed for my December conference. I was able to pay for my decorator and more as God provided the funds I needed. When you are obedient to building, God will fund it. My leaders prayed over me the final night that I spoke as my sister Lakia Perez stood behind me, and God moved powerfully as I ministered the word of God. Then, I went forth in individual prayer and prophesied and God moved powerfully.

Also, in December, I had this amazing opportunity to speak at Norfolk State University. My mentorship program grew, the Fire Academy was relaunched for the first quarter, and I also announced the launch of My Sister Helped Me Heal anthology.

God had set things in motion to begin 2022 strong, and my friends and I could sense that 2022 would be a year that God would do some amazing things in our lives. When I look back from the end of 2019 to 2021, I can truly say God has blown my mind, accelerated me into purpose, been a faithful God, and held me close. If it were not for his grace and unending love, I would not have made it this far. Let God be your everything and trust him with your life. He will never fail you.

Epilogue

Happy New Year
The Year of Double
The Year of Divine Alignment and Overflow

Whew, what a ride, right? This journey has been one for the books for sure - no pun intended. This is my story. The good, the bad, and the ugly. One thing I know is that all things are working together for my good.

Before I crossed into 2022, there was a sense that God was going to do some amazing things this year. I really have no idea what it will be, but there is a sense that it will be big. As I brought in the year by myself, I shouted and praised God for bringing me over. I have noticed a different level of his presence with me since the new year. God told me something that I will never forget about time. God said, "I am not confined to time, but I work in time." What does that mean? There are designated times that God has prepared to allow blessings, increase, expansion, miracles, and more. In 2022, some great things were reserved for this particular time. Think about it, Jesus came at a specific time, Esther was born for a time, and the list could go on. There are many things that I have built that have been a foundation for what I will continue to do.

The first two months of the first quarter of this year have been about establishing systems and processes for growth and expansion. There are so many things that I currently do. I can easily be pulled in many directions. God has given me time and strategy on how to execute the influx in this season. You must prepare for the rain, which is the abundance and the overflow.

After taking a break from social media at the end of January, God told me to host an event that I had planned for March to happen at the end of the month. I was like, okay God. The word that prophetess Deleigh preached and the way she prophesied to us at the one-night virtual conference was just what we needed walking into 2020. During this time, I was also going through the interview process with Regent University for the Student Success Manager position. In this position, I have the opportunity to lead the coaching department and help with other student matters for engagement and community building. I prayed, and I told God what I wanted. Although I left my job as a teacher, it was this position I was afraid to take before I resigned because of the pay difference. However, God ended up calling me off my job as a teacher to focus on business and ministry. I told the interview team at Regent that I felt more prepared to serve in the position I was not ready to accept last summer because of all the experience I had gained as an entrepreneur. Obeying God to leave my job as a teacher opened doors of opportunity in ministry, business, and now higher education. Some people may see this as a failure, but God showed me how working at Regent would make me better for business and ministry and allow me to share my talents with a new and larger audience in this season.

I told God that the position at a Christian educational institution over a coaching department was a dream job. I prayed, and I asked God to open the door for it to happen. God answered my prayer. I bring to the table all of me, and it is appreciated. It allows me to stretch myself as I build for an organization that is so much bigger than mine. We trust God to order our steps, and whatever shift comes in the future, I will be ready to follow his lead again. I truly believe that God is a good father that leads and directs us to where he wants us to be at every given time of our life.

Now, I am preparing for the celebration of an anthology for which I am the visionary for, called My Sister Helped Me Heal: The Power of Kingdom Sisterhood. The faith in God in the mountain tops and valleys of life allows me to serve God in all seasons of life. God is just getting started with me, and I am excited to be on this journey with him.

Choose to live an obedient life despite all that tries to kill you or cause you to cave under pressure. God is not done with you. God has a plan and purpose for your life that if you are willing to stay faithful to him, he will remain faithful to you. Understand that the road will not be easy, and that warfare will come your way. Yet, you must keep your eyes on God and your ears positioned to hear his voice. The best is yet to come. Don't settle for a life that others have expected you to live and even how people may try to box you in. Instead, choose to follow God's lead. He will blow your mind. The scripture that God gave me to apply to my life in 2020 still rings true today: Ephesians 3:20, "Now unto him who is able to do exceedingly abundantly about all you can ask or think according to the power that works within you." Shift, believe, transform, evolve, and pivot into purpose. Lean into the God who has established a plan for your life that you must lean into him to make sure you learn, grab, and then execute.

Meet the Author:

Chavon is an Amazon #1 International Bestselling Author, Transformational Speaker, Leadership and Life Coach, and Talk Show Host. She is the CEO of Purpose Unwrapped, LLC and non-profit Power and Grace Leaders, Inc. Also a board member- COO- of an Accreditation organization- Governing Council.

Chavon is affectionately known as the Fire Leadership Coach. She marries practical and spiritual tools to empower and equip kingdom people to lead in the world. Formerly a high school educator, her mission is now to help Kingdom people Break Fear, Build Faith, and Lead Confidently online and beyond. She believes it takes commitment, confidence, and courage to impact culture.

She is also a transformational speaker who speaks with great passion in a way that empowers and challenges her listeners. She has been featured as a speaker on ABC news, TCT Today, Virginia Wesleyan University, at conferences and other events such as the globally recognized Comeback Champion Summit and Sister Leads Conference.

Chavon has published four books that are available on Amazon, and she has been a part of seven anthologies. Three anthologies became Amazon #1 Bestsellers- Undeterred, (International Bestselling) Unveiled Transparency, Called to Intercede and Sister Leaders. Now, she is in the process of birthing out My Sister Helped Me Heal Anthology, where she is the visionary.

Chavon Anette was the 2021 Servant Leader of the Year Award Recipient from ACHI Magazine. Also, in 2021, she was nominated for ACHI as Entrepreneur of the year, mentor of the year, author of the year, and TV personality of the year. In 2018, Chavon was nominated for ACHI as Author of the year and Educator of the year. In 2019 she was nominated for ACHI as Educator of the Year and Orator of the Year!